NEW VANGUARD • 182

ITALIAN BATTLESHIPS
OF WORLD WAR II

MARK STILLE　　　　　ILLUSTRATED BY PAUL WRIGHT

First published in Great Britain in 2011 by Osprey Publishing,
PO Box 883, Oxford, OX1 9PL, UK
P1385 Broadway, 5th Floor, New York, NY, USA
Email: info@ospreypublishing.com

Osprey Publishing is part of Bloomsbury Publishing plc

Transferred to digital print on demand 2017

First published 2011
2nd impression 2013

Printed and bound by PrintOnDemand-Worldwide.com, Peterborough, UK

A CIP catalogue record for this book is available from the British Library

ISBN: 978 1 84908 380 5
PDF e-book ISBN: 978 1 84908 381 2
ePub e-book ISBN: 978 1 84908 831 2

Page layout by Melissa Orrom Swan, Oxford
Index by Auriol Griffith-Jones
Typeset in Sabon and Myriad Pro
Originated by United Graphic Pte Ltd

Acknowledgements
The author is indebted to the staff of the Naval History and Heritage Command
Photographic Section and to Tohru Kizu, editor-in-chief of *Ships of the World* Magazine for
assistance in procuring the photographs which appear in this book.

The Woodland Trust
Osprey Publishing is supporting the Woodland Trust, the UK's leading woodland
conservation charity, by funding the dedication of trees.

www.ospreypublishing.com

CONTENTS

ITALIAN BATTLESHIPS OF WORLD WAR II

INTRODUCTION

One of the most misunderstood aspects of the naval war in the Mediterranean is the role of the Italian Navy's capital ships. The commonly held perception is that they were committed only sparingly and, when faced with the British fleet, were always defeated. The actual story is far different and deserves proper attention. After entering the war, the Italians committed their battleships aggressively. Even after the disaster at Taranto, where several ships were placed out of action (but only one for the duration of the war), the Italians continued to employ their battleships as part of their strategy to retain control of the central Mediterranean. It was only late in the war, principally driven by fuel shortages, that the Italians ceased operations of their remaining capital ships. Ironically, the most dramatic loss of an Italian capital ship came at the hands of their former German allies when the Italians changed sides in September 1943. By the end of the war, three of the four rebuilt Italian battleships remained in service, together with two of the three modern battleships. This book tells the story of the seven Italian battleships that saw service between 1940 and 1943.

ITALIAN NAVAL STRATEGY AND THE ROLE OF THE BATTLESHIP

Between the wars, the *Regia Marina* (Royal Navy) considered the French Navy as its most likely opponent. Increasingly in the 1930s, as Italian foreign policy became expansionist, war with Great Britain was seen as inevitable. When Italy entered the conflict in June 1940 by declaring war on France and Great Britain, the *Regia Marina* was not ready for war. This did not matter to Italian dictator Benito Mussolini, who judged that he had entered into the final stages of a brief conflict and that Italy was on the winning side. Given this perception, the Italians were loath to risk their fleet. The generally cautious Italian naval planners were also driven by the fact that losses to the fleet, especially battleships, could not be readily replaced by Italy's weak maritime industry. Thus, in essence, the Italians had no incentive to risk their fleet in a short war.

Going into the war, the *Regia Marina* had several primary missions. Foremost was maintaining communications with Libya in North Africa and the Balkans. This required the movement of regular convoys to those areas. Another important task was the control of the central Mediterranean, thus denying its use to the British. This was a key strategic factor during the war, as it dramatically increased the shipping requirements to maintain British forces in the Middle East. Unable to use sea lanes through the Mediterranean, the British were forced to use the Cape of Good Hope route around Africa, a total distance of 12,000 miles. This quadrupled shipping requirements compared with the Mediterranean route and had strategic implications for Allied capabilities and plans worldwide. Instrumental to being able to move convoys to Africa and keeping the Mediterranean closed to Allied shipping was the maintenance of Italy's battle fleet.

Cavour leading *Cesare* in a line ahead in 1938. When the Italians entered the war in 1940, these were the only two operational battleships available to engage the British Mediterranean Fleet. (Naval History and Heritage Command)

However, even within this strategically defensive construct, the *Regia Marina* did anticipate employing its battle fleet against the British. Even in a short war, this was to be done as soon as possible, but only close to Italian bases in the central Mediterranean. The Italians did not foresee operations by their heavy units in the eastern or western Mediterranean. As the war became extended, the *Regia Marina* never abandoned these general intentions, except for a single foray into the eastern Mediterranean with disastrous results. While strategically the *Regia Marina* was essentially defensive, the Italians employed their battleships aggressively on the operational level to achieve their primary missions until the point where fuel shortages precluded operations by large ships. However, the fairly aggressive commitment of battleships on the operational level did not translate to comparable aggression on the tactical level, but overall it cannot be said that the *Regia Marina* cowered in harbor during the war.

By August 1940, both *Littorio* (foreground) and *Vittorio Veneto* were operational. Both are shown here conducting gunnery exercises. Together, these ships formed the most powerful battle squadron in the Mediterranean. (Naval History and Heritage Command)

ITALIAN BATTLESHIP DOCTRINE

The *Regia Marina* intended to fight its battles at extended ranges; in fact, most battles in the Mediterranean were fought in daylight with good visibility, which facilitated this doctrine. Several factors shaped the Italian desire to fight at extended ranges. Foremost was the superior range of Italian guns, which gave them the ability to engage at long ranges beyond the range of their enemies. Another key factor was the superior speed of all Italian battleships over their British counterparts. Theoretically, this permitted the Italians to keep the action at extended range. It also gave the Italians the ability to choose whether and when to break off an action. Finally, with the exception of their modern ships, the rebuilt Italian battleships possessed inferior protection compared with British battleships so this made the *Regia Marina* reluctant to close the range where British heavy units were more likely to deal punishing blows.

Italian doctrine for surface action called for fire to be opened at long range. Gunnery was conducted in a deliberate manner, with fire being adjusted after each salvo. Once the proper range had been found, the target would be engaged with rapid fire to inflict maximum damage. After the enemy force had been attritted, decisive combat at short range would ensue. Obviously this doctrine hinged on accuracy at long range. In the pre-radar era, it was difficult for any World War II navy to demonstrate consistent accuracy at extended range, but the *Regia Marina* was as good as any other navy in this respect.

The Italians had made little preparation for night-fighting and, if given a choice, preferred to end an action when darkness fell. This certainly held true for Italian battleships, which were not to be risked at night. This placed the *Regia Marina* at a severe disadvantage against the British, who stressed night-fighting.

NAVAL TREATIES AND ITALIAN BATTLESHIP CONSTRUCTION

The Washington Naval Treaty signed in February 1922 gave the Italians a tonnage allotment of 175,000 for battleships, comparable with the tonnage allocated to the French. The treaty set a displacement limit for battleships at 35,000 tons with guns no larger than 16 inches. These limits remained in effect until late 1936.

The end of World War I saw the Italians well under their maximum battleship tonnage. Only the unique *Dante Alighieri*, the two surviving units of the Conte di Cavour class, and the two Andrea Doria units were in service. Thus, the Italians were not required to scrap any of their existing battleships, and were actually permitted to build new units up to a total tonnage of 70,000 tons between 1927 and 1931. However, as long as naval budgets were constrained by poor economic conditions, and the French Navy made no move to build up to its allowed tonnage, Italian battleship construction was stagnant. The Italians chose to put their limited naval construction budget into heavy cruisers in the 1920s.

The *Dante Alighieri* was scrapped in 1928 and the two oldest units of the Cavour class were placed in reserve. In 1928, fearing reports of French construction of battleships, the Italian Admiralty asked the Naval Construction Office to submit plans for three 23,000-ton ships equipped with 15-inch guns. A subsequent design called for a ship with 16-inch guns. Since French battleship construction had not resumed, these plans were dropped, and a much larger design was chosen, which eventually became the Vittorio Veneto class.

The first Italian dreadnought was *Dante Alighieri*, launched in 1910 and commissioned in 1913. She was fast and well armed for her time, but was deficient in armor protection. The ship provided a template for the next two classes of Italian dreadnoughts. *Dante Alighieri* was taken out of service in 1928 and scrapped the following year. (*Ships of the World*)

The first Italian "super dreadnought" design was the Francesco Caracciolo class, which was intended to match the heavily armed fast battleships of foreign navies. The final design called for a 28-knot ship with eight 15-inch guns but with lighter armor than foreign contemporaries. The first of the four-ship class was ordered in 1914, but construction was halted during World War I. Construction on the lead ship, shown here, was resumed after the war, but never completed. The hull was scrapped in 1921. (*Ships of the World*)

In 1932, the French laid down the first of two 26,500-ton Dunkerque-class battleships with 13-inch guns. This prompted the Germans to respond with the two ships of the Scharnhorst class, and the Italians to respond with design work for what was to become the Vittorio Veneto class. The new Italian ships were much larger than the displacement of 35,000 tons required to adhere to treaty limits and were in fact over 40,000 tons. Concurrently with the planned construction of a new class of battleships, the modernization of the four older battleships was ordered as a stopgap measure to counter the new French battleships.

On October 28, 1934, the anniversary of the fascist "march on Rome," keel-laying ceremonies were held for the first Italian battleships to be built since World War I. These were the first two units of the Vittorio Veneto class. In 1938, no longer bound by any treaty obligations to restrict naval construction, two additional units were authorized and laid down. Overall, the system of naval treaties between the wars had a dramatic impact on the growth of capital ships. However, given the economic straits of Italy, this effect was least pronounced on the *Regia Marina*.

Roma fitting out in Trieste in 1942. She was commissioned in June 1942 and entered active service in August. *Roma* was the last battleship commissioned by the *Regia Marina*. (Naval History and Heritage Command)

ITALIAN BATTLESHIP WEAPONS

The main armament of Italian battleships was impressive on paper, especially the outstanding range and penetrating power of the new 15-inch gun. However, it is important to note that Italian battleship guns did not sink a single enemy ship during the war. The high muzzle velocity of the 15-inch gun caused excessive barrel wear, and therefore contributed to the persistent Italian problem of salvo dispersion. Maximum barrel life was some 120 rounds, much less than other nations' 15-inch guns. Dispersion was also increased by excessive manufacturing tolerances, both of the guns themselves and the ammunition they used. The salvo dispersion problem was even more prevalent for the re-bored 12.6-inch guns mounted on the four older battleships. These had a barrel life of only 150 rounds.

Characteristics of Italian Battleship Main Guns

Type	Classes	Maximum elevation (degrees)	Maximum range (yards)	Rate of fire (per minute)	Muzzle velocity (feet per second)	Shell weight (pounds)
12.59-inch/43.8-cal Model 1934, 1936	Cavour, Duilio	27	31,280	2	2,722	1,155
15-inch/50-cal M1934	Vittorio Veneto	35	46,216	1.3	2,854	1,951

Fire control for the main battery was comparable with that of other navies of the period. After World War I the Italians decided to abandon their existing fire control systems and buy a British Barr and Stroud system. This was licensed and produced in Italy and then fitted on the modernized Cavour and Duilio classes. Range was figured optically with the aid of a fire control computer. On the older battleships the main battery director mounted above the bridge structure contained two to four 23.6-feet-long paired rangefinders. On the Vittorio Veneto and Duilio classes, the director was a fixed structure above the rotating rangefinder. The rangefinders were stabilized to avoid training errors. The fire control director transmitted data below to the plotting room where a fire control solution was generated. The plotting table for the main battery plotted five different factors: range and bearing of the target, target course, target speed, and the range rate. The Italians preferred to engage a target at a deliberate rate allowing fire to be observed and corrected. During the war, Italian shooting usually proved to be accurate, but was marred by excessive salvo dispersion, a problem never solved.

The secondary armament aboard Italian battleships was universally of mediocre quality. The Italians considered a heavy secondary armament to be an important design feature since it was necessary to engage the large numbers of destroyers possessed by the French Navy. Because the Italians did not develop a reliable dual-purpose gun, their battleships employed the space- and weight-consuming design practice of fitting both a secondary battery and a dedicated long-range antiaircraft battery.

ABOVE LEFT
This view shows the aft 12.6-inch gun turrets of *Duilio*. The original guns were designed by the British firm Elswick. During *Duilio*'s reconstruction the barrels were re-bored to 12.6 inches which allowed the guns to fire a heavier shell at a higher muzzle velocity. However, this process reduced longitudinal resistance to barrel droop, which increased the problem of dispersion. (*Ships of the World*)

ABOVE RIGHT
Close-up view of the forward 12.6-inch gun turrets on *Cavour* following her reconstruction. Note the slogans *"Re"* (King) and *"Duce"* (Leader) on the turret sides. The top turret has twin 20mm/65 antiaircraft guns mounted on its roof. (Naval History and Heritage Command)

This close-up of *Littorio* shows the layout of most of her armament. This includes the two forward triple 15-inch gun turrets and one of the four triple 6-inch turrets seen between Turret Number 2 and the bridge. The six starboard 4.7-inch single antiaircraft guns are evident. Note the red and white air recognition stripes painted forward of Turret No. 1. (*Ships of the World*)

The 4.7-inch guns aboard the Cavour class were fitted in double turrets. They possessed a high elevation of 42 degrees, but could not be considered dual-purpose weapons. The 5.3-inch guns on the Duilio class were fitted in triple turrets and were designed to provide the same range as the earlier 4.7-inch guns with better dispersion. They also had a high elevation and were provided with antiaircraft shells for barrages against attacking aircraft. The 6-inch gun on the Vittorio Veneto class was also subject to a pronounced dispersion problem.

Characteristics of Italian Battleship Secondary Guns

Type	Class	Maximum elevation (degrees)	Maximum range (yards)	Rate of fire (per minute)	Muzzle velocity (feet per second)	Shell weight (pounds)
4.7-inch/50 cal OTO Model 1933	Cavour	42	20,779	6	3,117	52
5.3-inch/45 cal Model 1937	Duilio	45	21,435	6	2,707	72
6-inch/55 cal M1934	Vittorio Veneto	45	28,150	4.5	2,986	110

A close-up view of the bridge of *Cavour* in 1938 following reconstruction. The bridge was compact; on its top was the large rotating main battery director. This contained two 23.5-feet-long rangefinders (coincidence and stereo) as well as the pointer and trainer for passing information to the 12.6-inch gun turrets. (Naval History and Heritage Command)

The antiaircraft armament of Italian battleships proved to be a weakness. This was mitigated only by the fact that they did not face heavy air attack in their normal operating environment. Fire control of Italian antiaircraft guns was mediocre. Also, since most of the mounts were grouped tightly together amidships, the guns suffered from inadequate firing arcs.

The standard long-range weapon on the Cavour class was the 3.9-inch Model 1928 twin mount. It was based on a 1910 Skoda design and its performance was insufficient against modern aircraft. The Duilio and Vittorio Veneto classes were fitted with a state-of-the-art 90mm gun with a fully stabilized mount designed to fire 12 rounds per minute. However in service the stabilization system proved too delicate and the gun was prone to jamming. Combined with a high failure rate of the ammunition, Italian long-range antiaircraft protection was inadequate.

Characteristics of Italian Battleship Antiaircraft Guns

Type	Classes	Maximum elevation (degrees)	Maximum range (yards)	Rate of fire (per minute)	Muzzle velocity (feet per second)	Shell weight (pounds)
3.9-inch/50 cal OTO Model 1928	Cavour	85	16,610	10	2,886	30
3.5-inch/50 cal OTO Model 1938/1939	Duilio, Vittorio Veneto	75	17,440	12	2,820	22
37mm/54 cal Breda Model 1932/1938	All	80	4,360	120	2,624	3.5
20mm/65 cal Breda Model 1935	All	90	2,725	220	2,722	.66

Battleship light antiaircraft armament was also inadequate. The 37mm gun was mounted aboard all three classes with the Duilio and Vittorio Veneto classes carrying single mounts in addition to the normal twin mount. The twin mount suffered from heavy vibration problems, which obviously affected accuracy. The 20mm gun was fitted in twin mounts aboard all battleships. This mount could not train or elevate fast enough to track and engage high-speed targets.

ITALIAN BATTLESHIP RADAR

One of the greatest disadvantages suffered by the *Regia Marina* during the war was the inability of the Italian electronics industry to develop and produce modern radar equipment. At the start of the war, no Italian warship was equipped with radar. After a series of disastrous night engagements, culminating in the debacle at Matapan in March 1941, the Italians were forced to recognize that the Royal Navy was already using radar and that it put Italian warships at a severe disadvantage. Nevertheless, Italian industry was unable to provide a radar until late 1942, in other words after the decisive battles of the Mediterranean war. Only 12 sets were delivered before Italy's surrender in September 1943, of which the EC.3 "*Gufo*" (Owl) was the first to be deployed operationally. This set performed in a surface and air search capacity, but was primitive by Allied standards and performance was insufficient to permit radar-controlled gunfire. The Vittorio Veneto-class battleships were the first to be fitted with radar, and all three were so equipped by August 1943. They were mounted on the foremast or the top of the fire control tower. None of the older battleships received any radar before the Italian surrender. Performance of the EC.3 *ter* (the production version) was modest compared with Allied equipment. When mounted on a battleship, range against a surface target was approximately 16nm and against aircraft detection ranges of 50 miles were possible.

Explanation of the Names of Italian Battleships	
Conte di Cavour	Camillo Benso, 1810–1861, a leading figure in the movement for Italian unification and the first prime minister of united Italy
Giulio Cesare	Italian for Roman Emperor Julius Caesar
Caio Duilio	named after the Roman fleet commander Gaius Duilius
Andrea Doria	mercenary and admiral from Genoa (1466–1560)
Vittorio Veneto	a major victory against the Austro-Hungarian Empire in October–November 1918
Littorio	symbol of the Italian Fascist party
Roma	the city and empire of Rome
Impero	Italian for Empire, specifically the new Italian empire proclaimed by Mussolini after the conquest of Ethiopia

THE BATTLESHIP CLASSES

Cavour Class
Design and Construction

The first Italian dreadnought was the *Dante Alighieri*, which was completed in 1913. Her basic design set the tone for the next two classes of Italian battleships. *Dante Alighieri* stressed speed over protection and mounted a lighter main battery armament than her foreign contemporaries. The Italians assessed that the French were their most likely rivals in the Mediterranean, so when the French announced plans for two dreadnoughts in both 1910 and 1911, the Italians were prompted to respond with a new class of dreadnought. The result was the three-ship Cavour class.

The ships were designed in 1908, but the Italian shipbuilding industry did not complete them until 1915. By this time they were a generation behind the other naval powers of the day (with the exception of the French). The class was clearly deficient in protection, armament, and even speed.

The concept for the Cavour class called for a larger ship than the *Dante Alighieri*, which would allow for a greater scale of protection, addressing the principal design fault of Italy's first dreadnought. Because the Italians had no indigenous industry capable of building a main gun larger than 12 inches, they decided to retain a 12-inch gun designed by the British as the main armament for the new class of battleship. This put them at a disadvantage in terms of firepower since the British had already moved to a 13.5-inch gun, and soon would adopt the 15-inch, while the Americans and Japanese had adopted the 14-inch gun. Even the French had moved up to the 13.5-inch gun for their Bretagne class, which entered service in 1916.

Conte di Cavour shown as she appeared in World War I. The lead ship of the class was launched in 1911 but not completed until 1915 because of problems acquiring the required armor and 12-inch guns. The three ships of the class saw almost no service during World War I, but the *Leonardo da Vinci* was lost in 1916 after a magazine explosion. (*Ships of the World*)

A **THE CAVOUR CLASS.**

The top profile shows *Cavour* as she appeared during the battle of Punto Stilo in July 1940. The ship is in its prewar light-gray paint scheme. After being damaged at Taranto in November 1940, *Cavour* was later painted in a Claudus camouflage scheme in December 1941 for her transit from Taranto to shipyards in the Adriatic Sea.

The bottom profile shows *Cesare* in her splinter camouflage in the summer of 1942. In December 1941, the ship was given a Claudus scheme, but this was short lived. By summer 1942, a splinter scheme was adopted, which the ship wore until 1945. In 1943, the scheme was slightly modified, the primary difference being the addition of blue on the port side.

Both profiles show the overall layout of the Cavour class with its simplified bridge structure, the four 12.59-inch gun turrets and the secondary armament of three twin 4.7-inch guns amidships flanked by the two twin 3.9-inch antiaircraft mounts. Aside from the changing camouflage, the appearance of the ships was basically unaltered during the war.

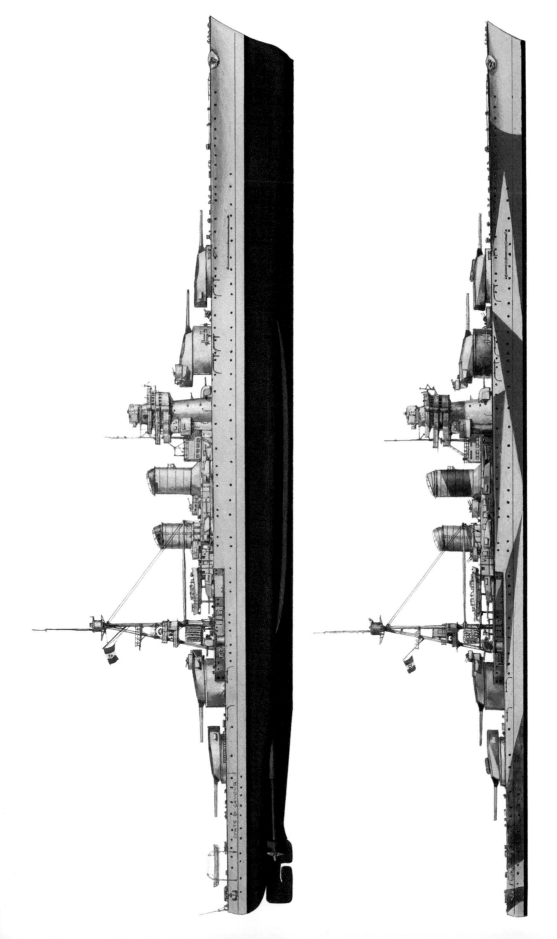

Cavour Class Construction

Ship	Built at	Laid down	Launched	Completed
Conte di Cavour	La Spezia Navy Yard	August 10, 1910	August 10, 1911	April 1, 1915
Giulio Cesare	Genoa by Ansaldo	June 26, 1910	October 15, 1911	May 14, 1914
*Leonardo da Vinci**	Odero	July 18, 1910	October 14, 1911	May 17, 1914

Leonardo da Vinci was sunk by a magazine explosion on August 2, 1916. Though she was raised in 1919 and plans were made to rebuild her, it was eventually decided to scrap her in 1923.

Protection was a design emphasis, but even when completed the ships were not as well protected as foreign rivals. The total amount of armor was 30.2 percent of design displacement. With this Italian designers provided a main armor belt 250mm deep with a width of just over nine feet. The main belt extended from the forward turret to the aft turret. The lower edge of the main belt was 170mm and the upper edge was 220mm, tapering to 130mm up to the main deck. The area of the bow was protected by a thin armored belt of 80mm and the belt at the stern was 130mm. Horizontal armor was divided into a main deck of 24mm sloping to 40mm on the edges and a middle deck of 30mm. Barbettes and the conning tower were covered by 280mm of armor. The five 12-inch gun turrets were provided with 280mm on their fronts, 240mm on their sides and 85mm on the roofs.

The original propulsion for the class was provided by three sets of turbines powering four shafts. Both ships employed mixed firing for the boilers. *Cavour* was equipped with 20 boilers (eight oil and 12 mixed coal/oil) and *Cesare* was fitted with 24 American-designed boilers, half oil-fired and half mixed-firing. Total output was 31,000 shaft horsepower (shp), which translated to a top speed of 21.5 knots.

Armament

As completed, the Cavour class mounted a main armament of 13 12-inch guns mounted in a unique mixed arrangement of three triple turrets and two double turrets. The two twin turrets were mounted in a superfiring position over the fore and aft triple turrets. The final triple turret was placed amidships with a restricted firing arc. The 12-inch guns were designed by the British firm Armstrong and produced in Italy.

The original secondary armament comprised 18 single 4.7-inch guns mounted in casemates, and 14 3-inch guns, most mounted on the tops of the 12-inch turrets. During World War I, *Cavour* and *Cesare* received a variable number of 76mm antiaircraft guns. From 1923 until the beginning of their rebuild, both ships mounted a secondary armament of 13 3-inch guns on the turret tops and another six 76mm antiaircraft guns mounted near the second smokestack. Three submerged 17.7-inch torpedo tubes were also fitted.

A port side view of *Cavour* in 1938 following her reconstruction. *Cavour* was virtually identical to her sister ship *Cesare*. (Naval History and Heritage Command)

Service Modifications

The Italians decided to modernize and essentially rebuild the surviving two ships of the Cavour class in 1932 and work began the following year. This was seen as a temporary counter to the new French Dunkerque class. The thinking behind this major investment was that it was cheaper than building entirely new ships. In the end, this proved to be false economy, because despite the fact that the work was the most extensive carried out by any major navy on a battleship between the wars, the result was still a unit with marginal capabilities compared with most other foreign battleships. On top of this was the additional drawback that the resources spent on refurbishing these old units could have been better spent getting the modern units of the Vittorio Veneto class ready for service before the start of the war.

Cesare shown after completion of her 1933–37 reconstruction. This view shows her new lengthened bow and the forward 12.6-inch gun turrets with the twin turret mounted in a superfiring position over the lower triple turret. (Naval History and Heritage Command)

The Italians were well aware of the protection and firepower deficiencies of these ships. Therefore, the decision was made not to simply modernize them, which would have produced only marginal capability improvements, but to rebuild them. This rebuild entailed leaving only 40 percent of the original ship, making this the most extensive of the battleship upgrade projects carried out by any navy between the wars. The rebuild of these units did improve their capabilities in all areas. Speed was increased considerably by lengthening the hull with a new bow that added another 33 feet to the ships' overall length and the replacement of the original machinery. Protection was also upgraded and improvements in firepower were realized as the existing guns were re-bored to 12.59 inches.

The modernization begun in 1933 added another 3,227 tons of armor to the original protection. Augmentation of horizontal armor accounted for most of this increase with main deck armor increased from 24mm to 80mm (100mm over the magazines), which now extended on both sides to the main belt. Turret

This view is aboard *Cavour* looking aft from the bow. The lower triple 12.6-inch gun turret weighed 733 tons with the superfiring twin turret coming in at 539 tons. Each turret could fire a salvo twice per minute. (Naval History and Heritage Command)

A stern view of *Cesare* after her reconstruction showing the after pair of 12.6-inch gun turrets. With the exception of minor alteration of her small-caliber antiaircraft guns, the ship was unaltered during the war. (Naval History and Heritage Command)

barbette armor was increased with the addition of an additional 50mm. Underwater protection, a key vulnerability from the pre-World War I design, was addressed with the provision of a new underwater protection system designed by Umberto Pugliese. This system added a hollow curved bulkhead in front of the 25mm torpedo bulkhead of between 10 and 50mm. The space in between was filled with hollow cylinders designed to absorb the energy of a torpedo explosion. The principle was that the hollow space would act as an expansion area to take the force of the blast instead of the ship's hull.

The modernization included an entirely new propulsion system. The old boilers were removed and replaced with eight superheated Yarrow boilers each placed in its own boiler room. New turbines were also installed, which increased power to 75,000shp. On trials, the ships developed over 93,000shp. Despite the increase in displacement from the modernization, the new top speed of both ships was over 28 knots. This was an important improvement as it made these ships much faster than the Royal Navy's modernized World War I battleships, thus giving the Italians the tactical advantage of superior speed.

The modernization resulted in an entirely new set of weapons. The triple 12-inch turret amidships was removed, leaving a main battery of ten guns in two triple and two twin turrets. Each of these guns was re-bored and their caliber increased to 12.59 inches. This allowed for the firing of a much heavier 1,157-pound shell. Elevation of the turrets was increased to 27 degrees, which produced a maximum range of 31,280 yards. A new secondary battery was fitted, which consisted of six twin 4.7-inch gun turrets and four twin 3.9-inch antiaircraft guns in shielded mountings.

During the war, no further modification was made to *Cavour* before she was sunk in November 1940. After she was raised and repairs begun, it was planned to give her a new secondary armament of 5.3-inch twin guns and

Cavour pictured from her port quarter in 1938 showing the arrangement of her secondary and antiaircraft batteries. The mainmast mounts a crane for handling the ship's boats. The Italians attempted to place a catapult on *Cavour* in 1937, but removed it after it was found to restrict the operation of the secondary and antiaircraft batteries. After this, neither Cavour class ship carried any aircraft handling facilities. (Naval History and Heritage Command)

Cesare had a long and interesting career. Launched in 1911, she saw almost no active service in World War I. Rebuilt before World War II (as shown here), she was actively employed from 1940 until early 1942. She ended her career in the Soviet Navy where she served from 1949 until sunk, probably by a mine, in 1955. (Naval History and Heritage Command)

a new antiaircraft suite including the new 65mm dual-purpose single mounts as well as radar. This was never completed before the Italian surrender. During the war, the only modifications to *Cesare* were two additional 20mm and 37mm twin mounts in 1941.

Fates

A review of the wartime operations of all seven Italian battleships is provided later, but the fate of each ship will be noted in its class section. *Cavour* was hit by a single British torpedo in the November 1940 raid on Taranto. She sank in shallow water but was raised and towed in July 1941 to Trieste for repairs. When Italy surrendered, she was scuttled in the shipyard on September 10, 1943. She was raised by the Germans, but sunk again by a US air raid on February 15, 1945. She was finally broken up in place between 1950 and 1952.

Cesare had a more active wartime career. She was struck by a single British 15-inch shell at the battle of Punta Stilo on June 9, 1940. Repairs were completed in seven weeks, but the ship was withdrawn from service in February 1942. From January 1943 she was assigned as a training ship at Pola until the Italian surrender in September when she escaped to Malta. As war reparations with the Soviet Union, she was handed over on February 3, 1949. She remained in Soviet service in the Black Sea until October 29, 1955 when she was sunk in Sevastopol harbor by an explosion under the forward part of the ship, which caused uncontrolled flooding and sank the ship in three hours. The cause of the explosion remains unexplained, but the most likely culprit was a German magnetic mine laid during the war. The tragedy cost 609 lives.

Cavour Class (after 1937 modernization)	
Displacement	
Standard	26,140 tons
Full load	29,032 tons
Dimensions	
Length (overall)	611 feet 7 inches
Beam	92 feet 10 inches
Draft	30 feet
Speed	27 knots
Range	2,472 tons of oil provided a range of 6,400nm at 13 knots
Crew	1,236 men

Duilio Class
Design and Construction
After the three ships of the Cavour were completed, the Italians still faced numerical inferiority against the French, who had five dreadnoughts finished or under construction. To address this situation, two ships of the Duilio class were authorized and ordered in 1911 with construction begun early in 1912.

In almost all respects, the design of the Duilio class was a repeat of the preceding Cavour class. The main armament was identical, but the secondary armament of the new class consisted of a heavier 6-inch gun. The protection scheme was also only slightly different. The main armor belt was still 250mm; the heaviest protection of 280mm was reserved for the turret barbettes, the turret faces, and the conning tower.

Dimensions of the two classes were virtually identical. The Duilio class employed a mixed coal-oil firing propulsion system that developed 32,000shp and a top speed of 21.5 knots.

Duilio Class Construction

Ship	Built at	Laid down	Launched	Completed
Caio Duilio	Cant di Stabia	February 24, 1912	April 24, 1913	May 10, 1915
Andrea Doria	La Spezia Navy Yard	March 24, 1912	March 30 1913	June 13, 1916

Armament
As completed, the Duilio class mounted the same main armament of 13 12-inch guns as the Cavour class. These were arranged in the same mixed layout of three triple turrets and two double turrets. The original secondary armament was increased from the Cavour class and comprised 16 single 6-inch guns mounted in casemates and 19 3-inch guns that could be placed in 34 different mounting points. Two submerged 17.7-inch torpedo tubes were also fitted.

Service Modifications
From entering service up until 1937, both ships received few modifications and none of these were major. The number of 3-inch guns was modified and in 1926 a catapult was fitted aft to launch a flying boat.

Duilio shown after World War I but prior to her 1937–40 reconstruction. The two ships of this class differed only in their secondary armament from the three preceding ships of the Cavour class. (Naval History and Heritage Command)

In 1937 both ships were taken out of service to begin a major overhaul. *Duilio* began work on April 1, and her sister ship followed one week later. The project was tantamount to a complete rebuilding and largely mirrored the work performed on the Cavour class. The rebuilding required that the amidships main turret be removed as well as all secondary and antiaircraft guns. The entire superstructure was also removed.

To address the weaknesses of the original design, the protective scheme was augmented to the same standard as that on the Cavour class with the exception of the barbette armor, which remained at 280mm. As on *Cavour*, underwater protection was improved with the fitting of the Pugliese protection scheme. However, as on the Cavour class, insufficient space was available to install the entire Pugliese system.

In order to increase speed, the original 20-boiler, four-shaft system was replaced with an eight-boiler, two-shaft configuration, which developed 75,000shp. This was adequate to increase the ships' top speed to 27 knots. The boilers were placed in four rooms, and these vented up through two smokestacks that were placed close together amidships. The ships' performance was also increased by the addition of a new 36-foot-long bow section which included a bulbous foot.

The deletion of the triple 12-inch turret amidships reduced the number of main guns to ten. These were arranged in four turrets with a triple and a dual turret each located fore and aft. As on the Cavour class, the twin turret was placed in a superfiring position over the triple turret. The loss of the amidships turret was compensated for by increasing the main gun caliber to 12.59 inches, allowing for the use of a heavier shell with better penetrating power.

The new secondary battery of the Duilio class was much heavier than that of the Cavour class. Four triple 5.3-inch OTO Model 1937 turrets were fitted, two per side all located alongside the rebuilt bridge structure. The aft triple

Despite her reconstruction, *Doria* (shown here) and her sister ship were little improved from the Cavour class. *Doria* presented a compact yet graceful appearance, but this belied her significant lack of protection. This placed her at a disadvantage when facing British battleships. (*Ships of the World*)

This 1940 image of *Doria* shows the layout of the ship after its reconstruction and the primary differences from the preceding Cavour class. While the main armament layout of the two classes was identical, the secondary armament of the Duilio class comprised two triple 5.3-inch gun turrets on each beam located abreast the bridge. The starboard heavy antiaircraft armament of five single 3.5-inch guns can be seen. Unlike the Cavour class, the bridge structure is larger, with a pole foremast immediately abaft. The mainmast aft is also a pole, as opposed to a tripod on *Cavour*. (*Ships of the World*)

Doria pictured after the completion of her reconstruction in October 1940. The ship was in Taranto in November 1940 during the British attack but was not considered combat ready and was undamaged. (Naval History and Heritage Command)

turret was placed in a superfiring position over the other. The class was fitted with an above-average antiaircraft armament for the period. Long-range antiaircraft protection was provided by ten 3.5-inch guns. These were placed in single turrets with five on each beam. The mounts were enclosed and fully stabilized, though the stabilization did not prove successful in service and was removed in 1942. Intermediate antiaircraft defense was provided by 37mm guns arranged in six twin turrets located near the smokestacks and the main mast, and three single guns on the forecastle in disappearing mounts. The light antiaircraft battery consisted of 16 20mm guns in eight twin mounts. Half of these were located around the main mast aft, and the others located on the two superfiring 12.59-inch gun turrets.

During the reconstruction, the original torpedo tubes were removed. The catapult was also removed. What resulted when the *Duilio* returned to service on July 15, 1940 and *Doria* on October 26, 1940 was a graceful ship, but one that still contained severe deficiencies. Compared with the British battleships they would face during the war, the Duilio class was faster, but was inferior in protection and firepower.

During the war, few additional modifications were carried out. Because Italian surface units did not face a severe air threat in the central Mediterranean, modifications to the antiaircraft battery were minor. Two twin 37mm mounts were added near the mainmast for a final total of 19 37mm guns. No additional 20mm guns were fitted. Of note, neither ship was fitted with radar during the war.

Fates

Duilio was damaged at Taranto, but was repaired by the end of April 1941. In 1942, both ships were laid up for lack of fuel in Taranto. *Duilio* and *Doria* proceeded to Malta when Italy surrendered and were returned to Italian control in June 1944. Thereafter, both ships were used as training ships, *Duilio* until May 1953 and *Doria* until mid-1956. *Duilio* was scrapped at La Spezia from 1959 to 1962 and *Doria* from 1959 to 1962.

THE DUILIO CLASS.

The top profile shows *Duilio* in April 1942 in her dazzle scheme. The ship remained in this attractive scheme until 1944. Previously, she was in a "fish-bone" scheme from spring 1941 until the adoption of the dazzle scheme in April 1942.

The bottom profile shows *Doria* as she appeared in December 1941 during the first battle of Sirte in her Claudus camouflage scheme. In April 1942 she was painted in a "lobed" variant of the splinter camouflage scheme.

The views readily show the differences between the Doria class and the Cavour class. While the placement of the main battery on both classes was the same, the secondary armament on the Doria class ships was greatly augmented, as shown by the five beam 3.5-inch antiaircraft guns and the two triple 5.3-inch turrets mounted abreast the bridge structure. The bridge structure itself was much more complex and both the foremast and mainmast present a different appearance.

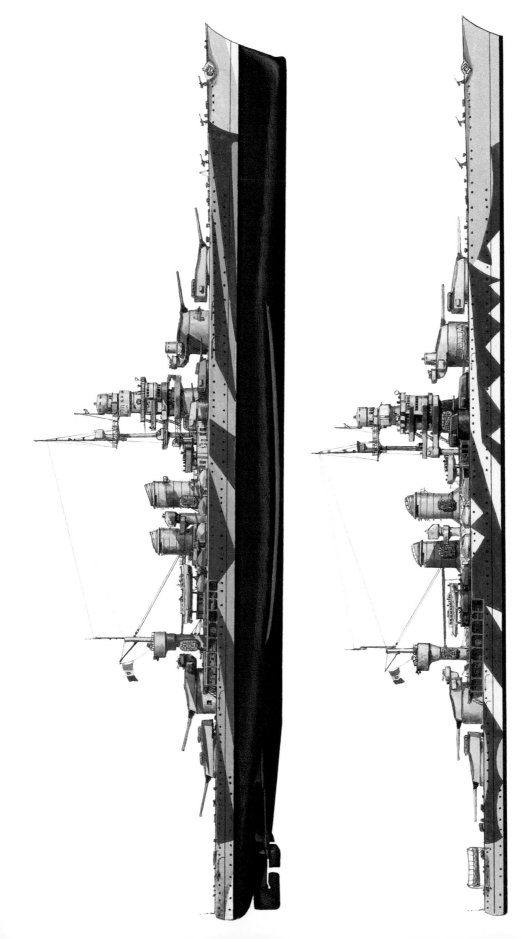

Duilio shown in the camouflage scheme she wore from spring 1942 until 1944. *Duilio*'s last combat operation was in February 1942 when she provided distant cover for a convoy to Tripoli, Libya. From mid-1942 the worsening fuel shortage forced the ship into inactivity, spending most of her time in Taranto until the surrender in September 1943. (Naval History and Heritage Command)

Duilio Class (after modernization)	
Displacement	
Standard	*Duilio* 26,434 tons; *Doria* 25,924 tons
Full load	*Duilio* 29,391 tons, *Doria* 28,882 tons
Dimensions	
Length (overall)	613 feet 3 inches
Beam	91 feet 11 inches
Draft	33 feet 10 inches
Speed	27 knots
Range	6,400nm at 13 kts with a maximum bunkerage of 2,550 tons
Crew	1,485 men

Vittorio Veneto Class
Design and Construction

With the French announcing construction of a new class of battleship in 1931, the Italians were forced to consider likewise. Original design specifications were for an orthodox ship of 35,000 tons armed with six 16-inch guns in three twin turrets and a speed of 28–29 knots. This design did not compare well with foreign designs and was rejected in favor of a modified design built around a main battery of nine 15-inch guns. Despite the smaller guns, this updated design provided a much heavier broadside than the 16-inch gun design. The driving factor behind the selection of the 15-inch gun was that an existing design from the never-completed Caracciolo class could be used; the design and production of a new 16-inch gun would have resulted in a delay of the start of construction of the new class.

Vittorio Veneto pictured in May 1940 just after completion. By any measure, the battleships of this class were handsome ships. Their combination of speed, protection and firepower was a credit to Italian designers and builders. (*Ships of the World*)

The new class of battleships was typical of Italian designs, which exhibited an elegant flair while maintaining a powerful appearance. The design was dominated by the three triple 15-inch turrets, two placed forward and one aft. The aft turret provided the class with its most recognizable feature since it was situated above the quarterdeck. The extra height created by placing the turret on a slightly higher elevation and lowering the quarterdeck one

Vittorio Veneto shown just after completion in April 1940. After fitting out, she sailed for Taranto in mid-May. When war was declared the following month, she was not yet operational. (Naval History and Heritage Command)

level was a design feature to protect aircraft on the quarterdeck from the blast of the main armament. The quarterdeck had sufficient room for a single catapult, an aircraft crane, and three aircraft.

The final design was a well-balanced ship with good protection, above-average firepower, and above-average speed. This was the first 35,000-ton ship to be designed under treaty limitations. Italian designers found that to meet the requirements of adequate armament, speed, and protection on a 35,000-ton hull was impossible. With the permission of Italian naval authorities, it was decided to design a ship of over 40,000 tons' displacement, a clear violation of existing treaty limitations. It should be noted that American, British, and French designers experienced the same difficulty of designing a well-balanced ship on 35,000 tons, and that all comparable foreign designs were also over this limit.

Vittorio Veneto Class Construction

Ship	Built at	Laid down	Launched	Completed
Vittorio Veneto	Trieste	October 28, 1934	July 25, 1937	April 28, 1940
Littorio	Genoa	October 28, 1934	August 22, 1937	May 6, 1940
Roma	Trieste	September 18, 1938	June 9, 1940	June 14, 1942
Impero	Genoa	May 14, 1938	November 15, 1939	Never

Littorio running trials in 1939. Not all of the ship's weapons have been fitted. She was completed in May 1940 but not considered operational until August. (Naval History and Heritage Command)

VITTORIO VENETO

The Vittorio Veneto class was the epitome of Italian battleship design. The ships presented an elegant and powerful appearance. This view shows the lead ship of the class as she appeared in summer 1941 in her "fish-bone" camouflage scheme.

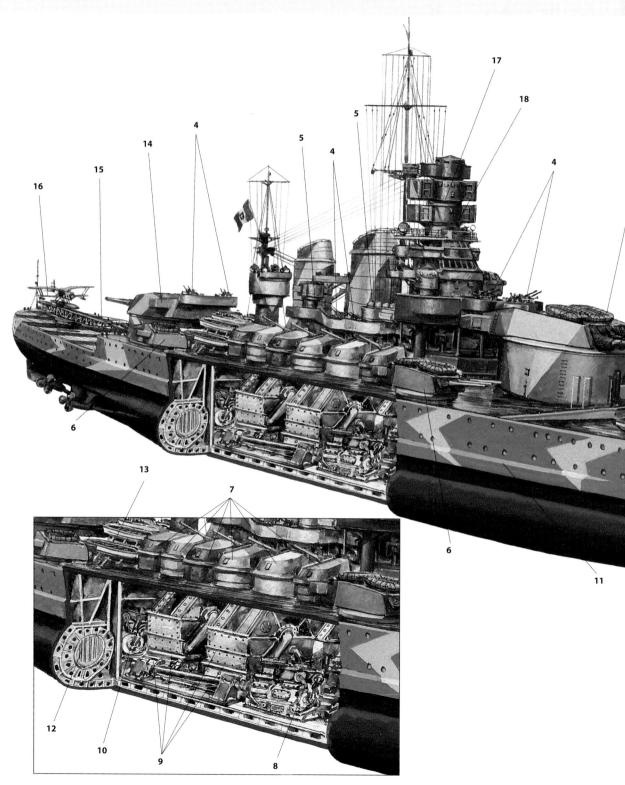

Key

1. 37mm/54cal Breda Model 1932/1938 single mounts
2. Number 1 15-inch triple turret
3. Number 2 15-inch triple turret
4. 37mm/54cal Breda Model 1932/1938 double mounts
5. 20mm/65cal Breda Model 1935 double mounts
6. 6-inch/55 cal m1936 triple mounts
7. 3.5-inch/50 cal OTO Model 1938/1939 single mounts
8. Forward starboard engine room
9. Starboard boiler rooms (four)

10. Aft starboard engine room
11. Main armor belt
12. Pugliese underwater protection system
13. Ship's boats
14. Number 3 15-inch triple turret
15. Catapult
16. Ro-43 reconnaissance floatplane
17. Main battery fire control
18. 23.6 ft. rangefinder for command ranging

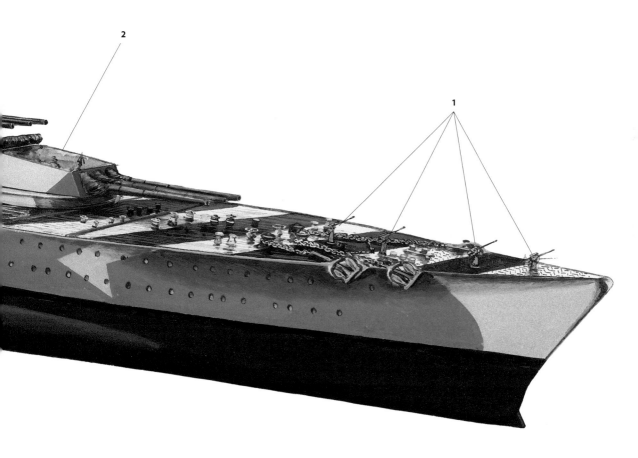

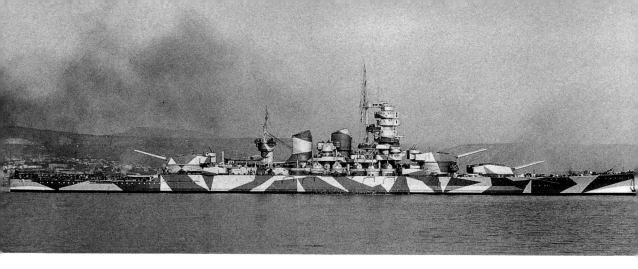

Roma in August 1942 shortly after her completion in June. The primary difference between *Roma* and her earlier sisters was the increased height of the bow, which can be clearly seen here. (*Ships of the World*)

Though the Italians were sure that the new design provided adequate protection against enemy battleship gunfire, the scale of protection was slightly inferior to other contemporary foreign designs. The main belt consisted of 280mm of armor with a 70mm outer plate and was 12 feet 4 inches deep, extending five feet below the waterline. This made the main belt relatively thin and shallow. Forward of the armored citadel the armor was reduced to 130mm and no side armor was provided aft.

Deck armor was comparatively heavy, but since these ships were designed in 1932, the horizontal protection proved inadequate during the war. Over the machinery spaces, the armor was a maximum of 169mm tapering to 156mm outboard. Over the magazines, this was increased to 219mm tapering to 166mm. Turret barbettes were covered with 150mm of armor. The conning tower was unlike foreign designs, which were built around a heavily armored conning tower situated low in the bridge structure. On the *Vittorio Veneto*, the entire bridge tower was provided some protection with the most armor fitted on the seventh through ninth level, where the captain's and admiral's bridges and fire control stations were located.

Unlike on previous Italian battleships, underwater protection was given special consideration and an elaborate protection system was devised and named after its designer, Umberto Pugliese. This consisted of an angled exterior belt covering the bulged lower hull and two interior longitudinal bulkheads. The semicircular space between the longitudinal bulkheads and the outer belt armor was an empty cylinder designed to act as a shock absorber. This space was filled with fuel oil, water, or a mixture of both, and the empty cylinder placed within it. The full force of an underwater explosion was designed to hydraulically crush the cylinder, thus dissipating its force. The same system was employed on the older battleships, but because the system could not be fully fitted on their limited beam, the Vittorio Veneto was the only class in which the entire system could be fitted. The system was designed to provide protection against 770 pounds of TNT. In service, it suffered from two defects. The first was caused by a manufacturing problem when rivets had to be substituted for welding since the rivets proved unable to handle the explosive stress placed on the seams. Additionally, the desire to maintain the required hull form for high speed meant that the maximum diameter of the hollow cylinder could not be maintained throughout the length of the area of the armored citadel.

Eight boilers were arranged in four boiler rooms. These drove four sets of turbines and created a maximum of 130,000shp to meet the design speed

Italian naval officers lead a group of foreign newsmen on a Vittorio Veneto class battleship in 1941. The group is on the port side of the quarterdeck; the large turret in the background is the No. 3 15-inch triple-gun turret. This view gives a good perspective of the height of the turret above the quarterdeck, a design feature to avoid blast damage to aircraft on the quarterdeck. (Naval History and Heritage Command)

of 30 knots. When the two lead ships ran trials in 1939, both developed greater than their design power and both reached over 31 knots with a displacement of over 41,000 tons. Even at full displacement in wartime conditions, they were able to make 29 knots. Trials did reveal a problem with the design of the bulbous bow, which produced hull vibration and caused flooding of the forecastle and heavy spray. The problem was rectified by adding a greater flare to the bow and lengthening it by five feet. *Impero* received this modification after launch, but since *Roma* was still building, the Italians took the opportunity to design a new bow that was five feet higher, providing greater sheer.

Three rudders were provided, with the main rudder located on the centerline and two auxiliary rudders outboard. These could operate together or independently, and provided good maneuverability and good redundancy in the event of damage.

Armament

The principal armament of the Vittorio Veneto class was the Italian-designed 15-inch gun, the first gun that size to be fitted on an Italian battleship. The 15-inch guns were fitted on three triple turrets. Each turret weighed 1,570 tons and was heavily armored with a face armor of 350mm with sides and roof of 200mm. Two turrets were placed forward, and the third aft. The aft turret was mounted on the aft end of the forecastle deck and overlooked the quarterdeck, where the catapult was located.

A heavy secondary armament was considered necessary and, accordingly, consisted of 12 6-inch guns fitted in four triple turrets. Two were placed on each beam and they shared the barbettes of 15-inch Turrets 1 and 3. The guns were 6-inch/55 with a maximum range of 28,150 yards. As was the case on earlier Italian battleships, this gun had a high elevation (45 degrees) but was not capable of antiaircraft fire. It was, though, provided with 252 rounds of high-explosive antiaircraft shells for barrage fire. *Littorio* mounted Model 1934 guns from Ansaldo while *Vittorio Veneto* and *Roma* were fitted with Model 1936 guns from OTO.

This 1942 image of *Roma* shows the aircraft handling facilities on the Vittorio Veneto class battleships. A small crane was fitted on the fantail to service the single catapult on the quarterdeck. There was room for three aircraft. (Naval History and Heritage Command)

Long-range antiaircraft protection was provided by a battery of 12 3.5-inch/50 cal Ansaldo 1938 or OTO 1939 guns. These were fitted six on each beam in single, fully stabilized mounts. Intermediate antiaircraft protection was provided by 20 37mm weapons mounted in eight twin and four disappearing single mounts. The twin mounts were placed amidships above the 3.5-inch battery and the single mounts were placed on the forecastle. Light antiaircraft protection was provided by 16 20mm guns. *Roma* was completed with 28 20mm in twin mountings.

The entire quarterdeck was devoted to operating aircraft. A 69-foot long catapult was placed aft, but no hangar facilities were provided for the three aircraft carried. One aircraft was usually carried on the catapult, and the other two were mounted on trolleys that were handled by an electric crane. When they entered service, *Vittorio Veneto* and *Littorio* each embarked three Ro.43 biplane floatplanes used for spotting and reconnaissance. The need for some sort of air defense prompted the Italians to experiment in 1942 with employing the Re. 2000 fighter aboard ships. This was a wheeled aircraft and had to land on a conventional airfield after launch. In September–October 1942, two each were embarked in *Vittorio Veneto* and *Littorio*. *Roma* received two in the summer of 1943 and *Vittorio Veneto* received a third.

Service Modifications

None of the ships of the class received extensive modifications during the war. Because of their restricted operations area and the fact that Italian ships were not under threat of heavy air attack, little was done to augment their antiaircraft protection. *Vittorio Veneto* and *Littorio* each received six additional twin 20mm mounts in the spring of 1942. These were placed in pairs on top of the Number 2 15-inch turret and the forward 6-inch triple turret, and the last pair abreast Number 3 turret. *Vittorio Veneto* later received another pair that was placed in the aft section of the superstructure.

These ships were the only Italian battleships to receive radar during the war. *Littorio* was the first when it received an experimental EC.3 *bis* in

D   ***VITTORIO VENETO* IN MARCH 1942**

These views show *Vittorio Veneto* as she appeared in March 1942 after the ship was painted in a dazzle camouflage scheme. This striking scheme was modified in August 1942 when the white sections of the bow and stern were painted light gray. In 1944, the splinter scheme was removed and the ship painted in a simple light- and dark-gray scheme.

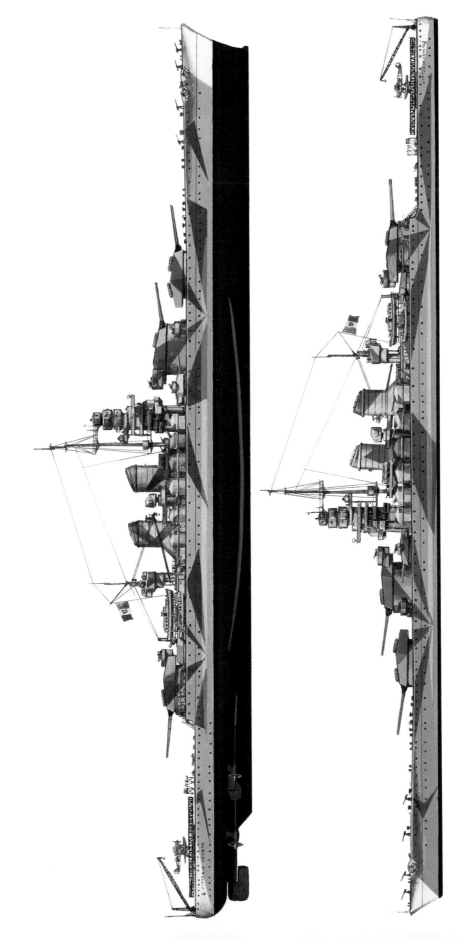

August 1941. In April 1942, she received an updated version. In September 1942, *Littorio* received an EC.3 *ter* radar. Before the armistice in September 1943, she had received a second set. *Vittorio Veneto* received an EC.3 *ter* in June 1943 followed by *Roma* in August.

Fates

Vittorio Veneto and *Littorio* both entered service in August 1940. Both saw extensive service up until Italy's capitulation and both ultimately survived the war. The lead ship *Vittorio Veneto* was torpedoed at Matapan in March 1941, but returned to service by August. She was again torpedoed by a British submarine in December 1941, but this time repairs took only three months.

Littorio was heavily damaged at Taranto in November 1940. On July 30, 1943, after the fall of Mussolini, she was renamed *Italia*. On September 9, 1943 she was badly damaged by a German glider bomb while transiting from La Spezia to Malta.

After being interned at Malta, both ships were moved to Lake Amaro (Great Bitter Lake) at the southern end of the Suez Canal in 1944. There they remained in internment until February 1946 when *Vittorio Veneto* was returned to Italy. She was ceded to Great Britain by the terms of the peace treaty with Italy but was returned to Italy for scrapping, which occurred from 1948 to 1950. *Littorio* was ceded to the US, but also returned to Italy before being scrapped at La Spezia.

Vittorio Veneto Class	
Displacement	
Standard	40,516 tons
Full load	45,029 tons
Dimensions	
Length (overall)	780 feet
Beam	108 feet 1 inch
Draft	34 feet 4 inches
Speed	29 knots at full load displacement
Range	3,966 (*Vittorio Veneto*) or 4,161 (*Littorio*) tons of oil provided a range of 4,700nm at 14 kts
Crew	78–82 officers and 1,750–1,760 enlisted, more if acting as fleet flagship; *Roma* 85 officers, 1780–1800 enlisted, when sunk total crew was 1,948

Roma entered service in November 1942, but was never deployed operationally. She was sunk on September 9, 1943 by two German glider bombs with the loss of 1,253 crewmen. *Impero*, after being launched in November 1939, was never completed. The incomplete ship was moved from Genoa to Brindisi, then to Venice and ended up in Trieste by September 1943. After the Italian surrender she was used by the Germans as a target ship before being sunk by a American air raid in February 1945. The wreck was scrapped in place from 1945 to 1950.

Littorio pictured in 1940, after her completion in June and before being damaged at Taranto in November. *Littorio* was the second most active Italian battleship during the war with 49 combat missions and a total of 32 days under way. (Naval History and Heritage Command)

ITALIAN BATTLESHIPS AT WAR

Though the *Regia Marina* was more ready for war than its sister services in June 1940, when the Italians entered the conflict the timing took the navy by surprise. The *Regia Marina* possessed only two combat-ready battleships,

The fourth ship of the Vittorio Veneto class was the *Impero*, launched in 1939 but never completed. Work on *Impero* stopped at the start of the war and the incomplete hull was in Trieste when Italy surrendered in 1943. Here the ship is shown under German control, who later used the hull as a target. On February 20, 1945 the hull was sunk by American bomber aircraft. (Naval History and Heritage Command)

Cavour shown firing a 12.6-inch gun broadside at the battle of Punta Stilo on July 9, 1940. The photo was taken from *Cesare*. During this action, both Italian battleships engaged the British at long range; both shot accurately, but scored no hits. (Naval History and Heritage Command)

and these were the oldest ships in the battle fleet, *Cavour* and *Cesare*. The first two modern battleships had already been launched, but would require three more months of training to be fully operational. Work continued on the two units of the Duilio class, with *Duilio* ready by the end of summer 1940, followed by *Doria* at the end of fall.

Despite their limited number of operational battleships, the Italians were eager to seek an engagement with the British. However, as would be the case throughout the war, the commander of the Italian battle fleet was ordered to accept an engagement only under conditions where the Italians held a clear superiority. The first clash was not long in coming and was one of the largest naval battles of the war. Like most battles in the Mediterranean, it was prompted by one side (or both) trying to move an important convoy through or into the central Mediterranean.

On July 9, 1940 the two sides met in the first fleet engagement of the Mediterranean naval war. This clash was called the Action off Calabria by the British and the battle of Punta Stilo by the Italians. The two available Italian battleships, *Cavour* and *Cesare*, sortied together with a combined force of 14 heavy and light cruisers and 16 destroyers. This force was covering a convoy en route to Benghazi. Once this convoy was deemed to be safe, the Italian battle fleet made course to engage the British Mediterranean Fleet with three battleships, one carrier and five light cruisers, and 16 destroyers. The action commenced at 1520 hours under perfect weather conditions. At 1552 *Cesare*'s guns opened up at 29,000 yards at British battleship *Warspite*. A minute later, *Warspite* returned fire at 26,000 yards.

E **CAVOUR CLASS BATTLESHIP *CESARE* DURING THE BATTLE OF PUNTO STILO**

When the Italians entered the war, only the two Cavour class battleships were ready for action. Their first action was at the battle of Punta Stilo on July 9, 1940. This view shows *Cesare* engaging the British battle fleet. All four of her turrets are trained to starboard and elevated for long-range fire. The Italian battleships opened fire at 29,000 yards, and though they shot accurately, no hits were scored. Later in the battle, *Cesare* took a 15-inch shell hit from British battleship *Warspite* and was forced to retire.

This photo shows the damage to *Cesare* at the battle of Punta Stilo after the impact of a single 15-inch shell from *Warspite*. The shell hit *Cesare*'s aft smokestack and detonated prematurely. The nose of the shell hit a 37mm shell magazine and a petty officer's mess but did not penetrate the armored deck. However, the resulting fire forced smoke into four boiler rooms, which forced the ship's speed to drop to 18 knots. With only a single effective battleship remaining, the Italians withdrew from the action. (Imperial War Museum)

At 1600 hours, a shell from *Warspite* hit *Cesare* at extreme range. The shell exploded prematurely on the smokestack and caused a fire. Smoke entered several boiler rooms, causing a drop in speed to 18 knots. With only a single battleship operational to face three, the Italian commander ordered a withdrawal. During the action *Cesare* fired 74 main battery rounds and *Cavour* another 41; no hits were scored. In the final phase of the action, the Italian air force made an appearance with 76 aircraft bombing the British fleet and 50 aircraft bombing the Italian ships. The battle proved to be indecisive, but many historians since have attributed a moral superiority to the British in its aftermath. Subsequent Italian operations proved this was not the case.

August 31, 1940, the Italian battle fleet, now with four operational battleships, 13 cruisers and 39 destroyers sortied to engage the Mediterranean fleet, which was at sea to escort a convoy to Malta. No contact was made when the British declined to engage this superior force. On September 7 the Italians again sortied, this time to engage British Force H based at Gibraltar. No engagement ensued as Force H had headed into the Atlantic, not the Mediterranean.

November 11, 1940, all six Italian battleships were at anchor in the naval base of Taranto in southern Italy. Such a target was too lucrative to ignore, and the British put into motion an operation to attack the Italian battle fleet with carrier-based aircraft. The base was heavily defended by antiaircraft guns, but no torpedo nets were in place and without radar the Italians had no warning of the approaching attackers. Gaining complete tactical surprise, the British torpedo bombers executed a skillful nighttime attack. Of the 20 aircraft participating, all obsolescent Swordfish biplane torpedo bombers, only 12 carried torpedoes (and only 11 were launched). Despite these meager numbers, the results were devastating. Three Swordfish attacked *Cavour*, and the first placed a torpedo just aft of the second turret. The others missed. *Littorio* was also attacked by three aircraft from the first wave and hit twice, once abaft the forward turret and the second time on the port quarter.

Another aircraft from the second wave hit *Littorio* on the starboard bow, which caused rapid flooding. Another torpedo struck her stern but failed to explode. *Duilio* was hit by her Number 2 turret, which caused flooding in the forward magazine and the ship to sink to the bottom of the harbor.

For the loss of two aircraft, the British temporarily reduced Italian battleship strength by half. *Littorio* was deliberately grounded in shallow water with her bow submerged up to the forward turret. She was raised and repaired in four months. *Duilio* returned to service by July 1941. *Cavour* was abandoned by her crew and the ship settled on the harbor bottom with her decks awash. She was refloated eight months later, but never again entered service.

Even after this devastating blow, the Italians showed no reluctance to initiate a fleet action against the British. On November 17, 1940 the Italian fleet sortied with *Vittorio Veneto* and *Cesare*, escorted by six cruisers and 14 destroyers. The objective was to intercept Force H from Gibraltar, which was conducting a mission of flying 12 aircraft to Malta. The British launched the aircraft early to avoid contact with the superior Italian fleet, and eight of the 12 aircraft were lost. The Italians returned to base after being unable to locate the British.

The myth of Italian post-Taranto timidity was again shown to be false when the supposedly crippled Italian battle fleet with *Vittorio Veneto* and *Cesare* departed Naples on November 26 to intercept a Malta-bound convoy from Gibraltar. Despite the fact that the Italian battle fleet outnumbered the convoy's escort, faulty air reconnaissance prevented the Italians from closing the convoy and provided an inflated assessment of British strength. After the losses at Taranto, the Italian fleet commander was under orders to be extra cautious. In a brief battle, cruisers on both sides engaged in an indecisive long-range gunnery duel. Finally, after surviving an air attack by eleven Swordfish, *Vittorio Veneto* joined the fight at 1300 hours when she opened fire at 32,000 yards. She fired 19 salvos, but scored no hits. The entire battle had been conducted at long range, and ended up indecisive.

ABOVE LEFT
This overhead view shows *Cavour* surrounded by fuel oil, heavily damaged and half submerged with a severe list to starboard. All this damage was the result of a single torpedo hit on the starboard side under the No. 2 12.6-inch gun turret. *Cavour* was the only battleship of the three damaged at Taranto not to return to service. (Imperial War Museum)

ABOVE RIGHT
Taken by British aircraft after the November 11, 1940 air raid on the Italian fleet anchorage at Taranto, this view shows salvage operations already under way on *Littorio*, which was struck by three torpedoes in the attack. The ship is down by the head with her entire forecastle awash up to the first 15-inch gun turret. By December 11, 1940 the ship was refloated and repairs were completed by the end of March. After refresher training for the crew, the battleship was again combat ready in June 1941. (Naval History and Heritage Command)

Another shot of *Littorio* following her damage at Taranto. As already indicated, *Littorio* returned to full service by June 1941. Another battleship damaged in the attack, *Duilio*, also returned to service by mid-June. Given this, and the fact the Italian battleships undamaged in the attack engaged the British fleet twice in November 1940, Taranto was not the decisive British victory that it is popularly believed to be. (Imperial War Museum)

January 8, 1941, an air raid damaged *Cesare* in Naples, leaving only *Vittorio Veneto* operational. A month later *Cesare* and *Doria* had both rejoined the fleet after completing repairs. On February 9, Force H bombarded Genoa with a battleship and a battlecruiser. The Italian battle fleet put to sea to intercept with all three operational battleships, three cruisers, and 10 destroyers. Bad weather hampered Italian air reconnaissance, and the British escaped.

The next fleet engagement was the result of the most aggressive major Italian naval operation of the entire war. The Germans had pressed the Italians to interfere with British shipping supporting their forces in Greece, and promised air cover if the Italians moved to interdict it. The result was the Battle of Matapan, when the Italians put to sea with *Vittorio Veneto* escorted by eight cruisers and 13 destroyers. The British had prior knowledge of Italian intentions and deployed the Mediterranean fleet built around three battleships and a carrier. The fleets met south of the eastern tip of Crete on March 28. As the opposing cruisers clashed, *Vittorio Veneto* came to full speed and engaged with her 15-inch guns at 25,000 yards. The battleship fired 92 shells with no success. However, before the weight of her salvos could be fully felt, six British torpedo bombers attacked her. No hits were scored, but the Italians reversed course. A second wave of carrier torpedo bombers later launched a well-executed attack from both sides of *Vittorio Veneto* and placed a single torpedo aft on her port side, which put the port shafts out of action and caused severe flooding. Damage control efforts succeeded in controlling the flooding and restoring power to the starboard shafts to allow

F   ### *ROMA* UNDER ATTACK

On September 9, 1943 *Roma* and her two sister battleships were transiting to Malta to be interned by the Allies. This scene shows the ship under attack by German aircraft using radio-controlled bombs just before she blew and sank with heavy loss of life. *Roma* is maneuvering at high speed and firing at her attackers. However, in just moments the ship was struck by one of the radio-controlled bombs with its 660-pound warhead and the chain of events began that caused 1,253 Italian crewmen to lose their lives.

Roma is shown in the dazzle camouflage scheme that she was completed in. The ship retains the red and white air recognition stripes on her bow and stern section. The appearance of the ship was almost identical to the earlier Vittorio Veneto class ships. The primary difference is the greater sheer of the bow, which can be barely discerned in this view.

for 10 knots. A third strike at dusk found the *Vittorio Veneto* steaming at 15 knots. The battleship was not damaged further and returned safely to port. However, one Italian heavy cruiser was damaged and forced to leave formation. Later that night the British battleships found the wounded cruiser and two other heavy cruisers detailed to escort her home and sank all three, plus two destroyers, by gunfire.

Vittorio Veneto was repaired by August 1941 and was joined by *Littorio*. *Doria*, *Duilio*, and *Cesare* were also operational, giving the Italians five battleships. All five ships moved to Taranto and the Italians sought to exploit this battleship superiority with a large-scale operation.

On August 23, *Vittorio Veneto*, and *Littorio*, four cruisers and 19 destroyers sortied to intercept a British force from Gibraltar on a mining mission off Livorno. The Italian battle fleet waited south of Sardinia, but no contact was made.

During the second half of 1941, the attention of both sides turned to the convoy war in the central Mediterranean. British advantages in code-breaking, and the reduction of Axis pressure on Malta making it an offensive springboard for British interdiction operations, put severe pressure on the Italians' ability to move supplies to Africa. Between July and December 1941, shipments to Africa dropped from 94 percent of cargoes reaching their destination during the first half of the year to 73 percent. Concurrent with the British interdiction of Italian convoys headed to Africa, the British had to keep Malta supplied. In September 1941, the Italian battle fleet was active against a British convoy to Malta. The convoy left Gibraltar on September 24 and was provided with an extra-heavy escort of three battleships including the 16-inch-gun-equipped *Nelson* and *Rodney*, and the British counterpart to the Vittorio Veneto class, the new battleship *Prince of Wales*. The Italian battle fleet, with *Vittorio Veneto* and *Littorio*, five cruisers, and 14 destroyers, put to sea on September 26, but again Italian air reconnaissance was faulty and reported that the British were too strong to engage. Following orders not to engage unless he possessed a clear superiority, the Italian commander returned to Naples.

The worsening supply situation in Africa forced the *Regia Marina* to commit its heavy ships to ensure that convoys arrived safely. On December 13 the two modern Italian battleships again sortied to provide distant cover

for an important convoy to Tripoli. Close support to the convoy was provided by *Duilio*. The convoy was recalled after a British submarine attack that sank two freighters, and as the Italian forces returned to port, *Vittorio Veneto* was torpedoed by a submarine in the Strait of Messina. One of three torpedoes fired hit the ship on the port side abreast the after turret. Despite the fact that the ship took on over 2,000 tons of water, she returned to port. Repairs were not completed until June 1942.

Two days later the Italians mounted another major convoy operation. The seriousness of the situation was indicated by the fact that the Italians committed their entire battle fleet to ensure the convoy's safe passage. The close covering force included *Duilio* and distant support was provided by a force built around *Littorio*, *Doria*, and *Cesare*. At the same time the British also mounted a convoy operation from Alexandria to Malta. This prompted the first battle of Sirte on December 17, 1941. The British convoy was spotted by Italian aircraft and the Italian distant covering force was sent to engage it. After some confusion, and wishing to avoid a night action, the Italian commander did not engage the convoy's escort until the evening, when he opened fire at extreme range (35,000 yards) with *Littorio*'s 15-inch guns, followed by the other battleships. The action was halted by darkness and neither side suffered major damage. At the end of this confusing action, the four Axis freighters reached their destinations safely despite the best British attempts to intercept them, so the action must be seen as a success for the *Regia Marina*.

By March 1942 food levels on Malta were becoming critical and the British decided to mount a major operation to relieve the island. This resulted in the second battle of Sirte. On March 21 a British convoy was spotted heading west to Malta. *Littorio*, three cruisers, and eight destroyers were dispatched to engage. The action was fought under storm conditions and in poor light conditions. *Littorio* played a key part in the battle, firing 181 rounds of 15-inch shells and repulsing an attack by British destroyers. She did suffer minor damage aft when the blast of her main battery set one of the aircraft on her quarterdeck on fire and she was hit aft by a 4.7-inch shell. The Italians were unable to engage the convoy itself, but shot better throughout the battle and suffered little damage in return. Most importantly, the aggressive attempts to engage the convoy forced it to move to the south

This wartime photo from the Italian press can be identified as *Littorio* by the camouflage scheme she wore from the spring of 1942 until after the Italian surrender. The shot was probably taken in 1942, since the ship spent most of 1943 inactive. The power of the Vittorio Veneto class battleships is clearly shown in this view. Just the existence of these ships affected Allied naval strategy in the Mediterranean and beyond. (Naval History and Heritage Command)

This 1942 British aerial reconnaissance photo shows *Cesare*; it was almost certainly taken of the ship moored in Taranto where she was inactive throughout the year. The overhead view gives a good view of the arrangement of the ship's main armament and the irregular shape of the secondary 4.7-inch twin gun turrets, which were very cramped for the gun crew. (Naval History and Heritage Command)

Roma pictured soon after entering service in the summer of 1942. By the time she entered service, the *Regia Marina* was experiencing a crippling fuel shortage and was increasingly unable to match the combined naval might of the Allies. Accordingly, *Roma* was the least active of the Italian battleships with only 17 combat missions and a total of just over four days under way. (Naval History and Heritage Command)

and eventually to scatter in an attempt to reach Malta singly. This meant that the ships were still at sea and exposed to air attack the next day. Ultimately, only a small fraction of the convoy's cargo was salvaged, thus making the battle another victory for the Italians.

In the summer of 1942 *Vittorio Veneto* returned to service and the *Roma* began trials in June. Meanwhile, the situation on Malta was increasingly desperate. In June 1942, the British mounted the largest operation to date to relieve Malta. A six-ship convoy attempted to reach Malta from the west while another convoy of 11 ships departed Alexandria. The Italians were aware of British preparations for this operation and correctly judged the eastern convoy would be the main effort. On 14 June, the Italians directed *Vittorio Veneto* and *Littorio*, four cruisers, and 12 destroyers to attack the larger convoy. On June 15 the two battleships came under heavy air attack while en route to the expected interception point of the convoy. The only hit during the morning was a bomb hit on *Littorio*'s forward turret by American B-24s that did no significant damage. However, in the evening, a British torpedo bomber succeeded in putting a torpedo into *Littorio*. This hit on the forward starboard side and resulted in over 1,500 tons of water entering the ship. Even facing only a single Italian battleship, the British convoy was forced to return to Alexandria since the Italian battle fleet out-gunned the

This photo shows the spectacular end of *Roma* on September 9, 1943. The second of two Fritz-X radio-controlled bombs hit the ship in the forward engine room, which caused fires that spread to the forward magazine. The resulting explosion, shown here, blew Turret No. 2 overboard. The ship later capsized and broke in two with heavy loss of life. (*Ships of the World*)

convoy escort. The mere threat of an Italian battleship had gained a major victory for the Axis.

By this point, the *Regia Marina* faced a severe shortage of fuel, which precluded operations by battleships. Thus, the climactic convoy battle in August 1942 prompted by a massive British relief of Malta faced only the threat of Italian cruiser opposition. As a result of the fuel crisis, only the units of the Vittorio Veneto class remained operational, and only enough fuel remained for critical missions. The three older units were placed in reserve. In November, the modern units were moved from Taranto to Naples, and in December were moved to La Spezia. By the end of the year, the older battleships were taken out of service.

For the remainder of the war, the *Regia Marina*'s battleships saw no further action and were reduced to hiding in-port trying to avoid air attack. On June 14, 1943, an Allied air raid placed one bomb on the port side near Turret 2 on *Littorio*. The damage was repaired at La Spezia. A later raid on June 5 put two bomb hits on *Vittorio Veneto*'s forward port side; the Italians were lucky since one bomb was a dud and the other caused relatively minor damage. *Vittorio Veneto* was sent to Genoa for repairs and subsequently returned to La Spezia. *Littorio* suffered light damage in the same raid, but was repaired at La Spezia. The *Roma* was also hit by two bombs in the June 5 raid, which caused severe flooding forward. On the night of June 23–24, two more bombs hit *Roma* aft. Damage was relatively minor, but the ship was sent to Genoa for repairs, which were completed quickly and the ship was back at La Spezia by August 13.

Sailors of the British battleship *Warspite* man the rails as the Italian battle fleet steams into Malta on September 10, 1943. The leading ship is the light cruiser *Eugenio di Savoia* followed by *Vittorio Veneto* and *Italia* (formerly *Littorio*). The two battleships spent the remainder of the war interned in the Great Bitter Lake and did not return to Italy until 1947. (Naval History and Heritage Command)

Meanwhile, events were moving quickly, which would force Italy out of the Axis coalition. On June 10 the Allies landed on Sicily. *Roma* and *Littorio* were available, but were not used in a futile attempt to repel the landings. It was decided to take *Doria* and *Duilio* out of reserve for reactivation; both were located at Taranto and the work would take two months. *Cesare* was assigned to the naval school in Pola.

On July 25 Mussolini's Fascist regime fell. By this time the Italians were clearly looking for an exit from the war, but an armistice was not arranged until September 8, 1943. The battle fleet was held in reserve as a bargaining chip during armistice negotiations. Should an armistice not be reached, the fleet was ready to conduct a final attack on Allied landings on the Italian mainland. This would have been a near-suicidal operation as the battle fleet would have to transit over 500 miles from La Speiza with no air cover to face a superior Allied fleet.

Following the declaration of an armistice, the *Regia Marina* ordered all units to move to Allied controlled ports. On September 9, 1943 *Vittorio Veneto*, *Littorio*, and *Roma* were attacked off La Maddalena, Sardinia by German Do-217 aircraft carrying a radio-controlled bomb known as the "Fritz-X." When dropped from sufficient height, this World War II-era guided missile could penetrate battleship deck armor. *Littorio* was hit by a single bomb on the starboard side abaft the forward turret. Luckily for the Italians, the bomb penetrated the side of the ship and exploded in the sea close aboard. Another bomb hit close aboard on the port quarter, but *Littorio* survived to reach Malta.

Roma was much less fortunate and the attack brought an end to her short and tragic career. The first of two bombs to hit struck her starboard side and penetrated the Pugliese system to explode under the hull. The aft engine room and two boiler rooms flooded. Electrical fires caused a sudden loss of power and *Roma* was forced to leave the formation. The second bomb proved fatal. This also hit on the starboard side, and probably entered the forward engine room. The resulting fires spread to the magazine for the No. 2 turret, which soon exploded blowing the turret overboard. The ship continued to flood, and listed to starboard before capsizing and breaking in two. Of the 1,849 crew, only 596 survived.

Doria and *Duilio* proceeded from Taranto to Malta with no damage from attack. *Cesare* also sortied to Malta from the naval school at Pola, but en route a portion of the crew mutinied and attempted to scuttle the ship. The officers regained control and the ship arrived in Malta. The *Regia Marina*'s final two battleships, *Impero* and *Cavour*, remained in Trieste. *Cavour* was still six months away from completion of her repairs and *Impero* was only 28 percent complete overall.

Italian World War Two Battleship Camouflage

In 1931 the *Regia Marina* issued instructions on ship painting. Horizontal surfaces were painted in a dark gray (similar to the US Navy's dark gray) and all vertical surfaces were painted in light gray (just a little lighter than US Navy haze gray). Wood decks were kept in their natural color. This is the scheme that Italian battleships went to war in.

In the first major battle of the war, the battle of Punta Stilo in July 1940, Italian aircraft bombed Italian warships. This prompted the Italians to introduce a scheme to aid identification from the air. On the forecastle, wide red and white stripes were painted in a pattern descending from port to starboard. On battleships, the stripes extended from the bow to the area of Turret 1. At least the Vittorio Veneto class battleships had stripes on the quarterdeck as well. This was maintained up until the armistice. The tops of smokestacks, previously black, were painted light gray to make the ships less conspicuous.

In early 1941, tests were conducted on camouflage patterns for Italian ships. One of the patterns was adopted for *Vittorio Veneto*, *Littorio*, and *Duilio*. This was the so-called "fish-bone" pattern, which featured superimposed triangles painted in a shade of yellow-green. Deck surfaces remained dark gray, but wooden decks were now painted dark gray as well. This pattern was discontinued at the beginning of 1942.

Another pattern was devised by the well-known naval painter Rudolf Claudus. These schemes were designed to alter a ship's appearance as well as its course and speed. His schemes employed "sawtooth" patterns and used many colors. The Claudus schemes were used on *Cesare* and *Doria*.

The *Regia Marina*'s Technical Department issued detailed camouflage regulations in December 1941. By mid-1942, all Italian warships were camouflaged in dazzle patterns that focused on two colors – light gray and dark gray. Decks remained in dark gray and the air recognition red and white stripes also remained in use. Each ship had its own scheme and each scheme included one of three basic designs – lobed, straight-edged, and splotch patterns. The two colors of gray were never blended, but were clearly demarcated. Originally the extreme bow and stern areas were painted white, but this proved too conspicuous in the Mediterranean, so by August 1942 the white was replaced with light gray. Blue was also used on some areas.

ANALYSIS AND CONCLUSION

Technically and operationally, the *Regia Marina*'s battleships offered a mixed story of success. Technically, the decision to reconstruct the four older ships was a poor choice given Italy's limited construction funds and shipyard resources. Despite the fact that the ships were essentially rebuilt, the end result was ships with limited firepower and questionable protection. While the decision to convert the first two ships was perhaps defensible on the grounds

Doria in the camouflage scheme she wore from April 1942 until after the Italian surrender. Because her last combat operation was in January 1942, this shot was likely taken during the movement of *Doria* from Taranto to Malta on September 9, 1943. The ship remained interned in Malta until June 1944 when she was allowed by the Allies to return to Italian waters. (Naval History and Heritage Command)

that they provided some stopgap capability, the decision to rebuild the second pair of old battleships made little sense. All factors considered, the rebuilt battleships proved of little worth during World War II.

On the other hand, the design of the Vittorio Veneto class was a good combination of firepower, speed, and protection. These ships generally performed well in service. However, several weaknesses were apparent. Protection remained a weakness, particularly against underwater threats. The Pugliese system proved generally successful against torpedoes, but against non-contact explosions (like the one under *Roma*'s hull), the system failed. The biggest weakness was with horizontal protection, which was a direct factor in the loss of *Roma*. The deck armor layout was inefficient since it relied on two primary armored decks.

The continuing protection problems were exacerbated by damage control issues. Damage control equipment was inadequate; in particular, control of flooding was an issue because the fore and aft pump rooms were located outside the armored citadel and thus were vulnerable. Combined with the lack of portable power-driven pumps, this made the ships vulnerable to flooding. This was demonstrated at Matapan when the single torpedo that hit *Vittorio Veneto* almost led to the ship's loss due to progressive flooding.

Overall, the *Vittorio Veneto* was a good design, especially considering it was the first of the 35,000 treaty battleships.

Operationally, Italian battleships were well employed and were a crucial aspect of what was a largely successful naval war waged by the *Regia Marina*. The Italians were able to achieve their primary objectives in the Mediterranean

G   **LITTORIO IN JUNE 1942**

Littorio was the sister ship of *Vittorio Veneto*. These views show the ship as she appeared in June 1942. *Littorio* was virtually identical to *Vittorio Veneto*, with the exception of the placement of some light antiaircraft mounts. The ship is in a "lobed" variant of the splinter camouflage scheme that she maintained through 1943. Previously, *Littorio* was given a "fish-bone" scheme from March 1941 until spring 1942.

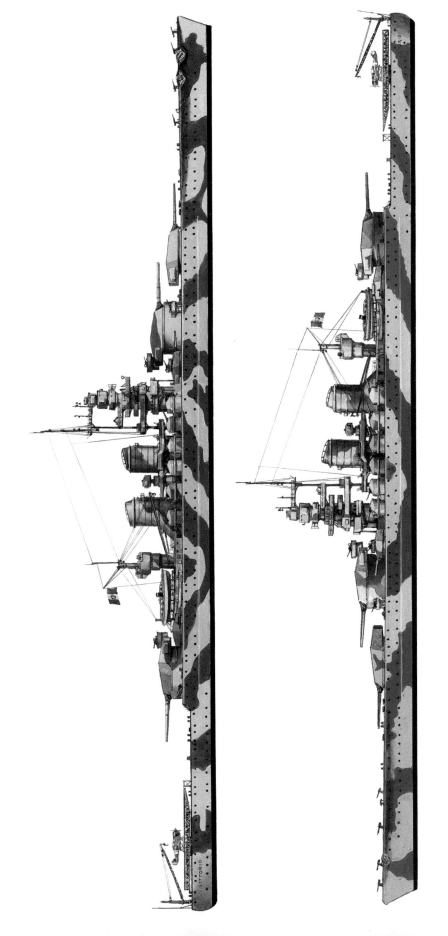

This view shows *Roma* in 1943. She received no modifications during her short life and carried the same camouflage scheme from completion until her loss 15 months later. (*Ships of the World*)

by holding open the sea lanes to Libya and the Balkans until May 1943 while simultaneously denying the Allies transit of the central Mediterranean until August.

Several themes were evident in Italian battleship operations from 1940 to 1943. Operationally, the Italians were eager to commit their heavy units and engage the British fleet. Tactically, it was a much different story with the battle fleet acting under orders to engage only an inferior force. This, combined with the existing Italian doctrine of engaging at long range, meant that almost all Mediterranean naval actions were indecisive. On top of this, the Italian admirals had to function under a system where effective naval–air cooperation was all but impossible. The lack of effective air reconnaissance was a constant limiting factor and several times prevented the *Regia Marina* from translating a numerical advantage into a potentially favorable tactical situation.

Italian battleships fought under other difficulties. They were especially vulnerable to air attack since land-based fighter cover was rarely delivered and their own antiaircraft capabilities were so weak. The lack of radar precluded any thought of a night engagement. As has been discussed, the effectiveness of battleship gunnery was greatly affected by the dispersion problem. Finally, the lack of reliable fuel supplies spelled an end to all combat operations.

Nevertheless, in the convoy war, 98 percent of Axis personnel were delivered safely to ports in Africa and the Balkans together with 90 percent of material. So, by this measure, the battleships, as the centerpiece of this exercise in seapower, were effective. When Italy surrendered, six of the seven battleships in service during the war were still afloat and operational. Thus, the *Regia Marina* avoided the fate of the other Axis navies that were virtually annihilated during the war.

BIBLIOGRAPHY

Bagnasco, Erminio and Brescia, Maurizio, *La Mimetizzazione Della Navi Italiane 1940–1945 (Italian Navy Camouflage 1940–1945)*, Tuttostoria, Parma, Italy (2006)

Bagnasco, Erminio and Grossman, Mark, *Regia Marina: Italian Battleships of World War Two*, Pictorial Histories Publishing Company, Missoula, Montana (1986)

Bragadin, Marc' Antonio, *The Italian Navy in World War II*, Naval Institute Press, Annapolis, MD (1957)

Breyer, Siegfried, *Battleships and Battle Cruisers 1905–1970*, Doubleday and Company, New York (1973)

Campbell, John, *Naval Weapons of World War Two*, Naval Institute Press, Annapolis, MD (2002)

Cernuschi, Enrico and O'Hara, Vincent P., "Taranto: the Raid and the Aftermath" in *Warship 2010*, Conway, London (2010)

Dulin, Robert and Garzke, William, *Battleships: Axis and Neutral Battleships in World War II*, Naval Institute Press, Annapolis, MD (1985)

Fraccaroli, Aldo, "The *Littorio* Class" in *Warship, Vol. I*, Conway, London (1977)

Friedman, Norman, *Naval Firepower*, Naval Institute Press, Annapolis, MD (2008)

Friedman, Norman, *Naval Radar*, Conway, London (1981)

Giorgerini, Giorgio, "The *CAVOUR* and *DUILIO* Class Battleships" in *Warship, Vol. IV*, Conway, London (1980)

Gregor, Rene, *Battleships of the World*, Naval Institute Press, Annapolis, MD (1997)

Ireland, Bernard, *Jane's Battleships of the 20th Century*, HarperCollins Publishers, New York (1996)

McLaughlin, Stephen, "The Loss of the Battleship Novorossiisk: Accident or Sabotage" in *Warship 2007*, Conway, London (2007)

O'Hara, Vincent P., "The Action off Calabria and the Myth of Moral Ascendancy" in *Warship 2008*, Conway, London (2008)

O'Hara, Vincent P., "Italy: The *Regia Marina*" in *On Seas Contested: The Seven Great Navies of World War II*, Naval Institute Press, Annapolis, MD (2010)

O'Hara, Vincent P., *Struggle for the Middle Sea*, Naval Institute Press, Annapolis, MD (2009)

Sadkovich, James P., *The Italian Navy in World War II*, Greenwood Press, Wesport, Connecticut (1994)

Whitley, M.J., *Battleships of World War Two*, Naval Institute Press, Annapolis, MD (1998)

Cesare shown in the camouflage scheme, which she wore between December 1941 and spring 1942. *Cesare* was very active from the start of the war through January 1942 when the Italians' fuel shortage forced her out of action. That December she was laid up at Pola where she remained until the Italian surrender. (*Ships of the World*)

INDEX

Note: Page numbers in bold refer to illustrations